W9-BRC-299

"STILL LIFE WITH THREE PUPPIES"
IS LIKE A LARGE SUN WITH A SERIES
OF MOONS LYING ABOUT ITS SURFACE.
THE ARTIST KEEPS OUR EYES MOVING
IN A SYMPHONY OF CIRCULAR PATTERNS.

PUPPIES' HEADS
AND THE ROUND POT.

GLASS TOPS AND

GLASS BOTTOMS WITH 3 FRUIT,

FRUIT AND FRUITBOWL,

AND

NAPKIN COVERED DISH. THEN NOTICE STILL ANOTHER CIRCLE

FORMED BY THE PUPPIES' TAILS AND THE ROUND POT HANDLE.
PAUL GAUGUIN HAS PAINTED A GAY UNIVERSE OF CIRCLES.

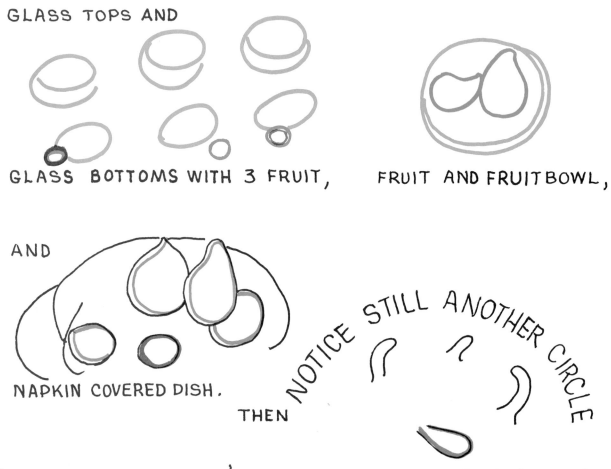

THE WHITE HORSE　　　　　　　　　　　　　　　　　　THE LOUVRE, PARIS

DEDICATED TO FREDRICK M. NICHOLAS

A GOOD FRIEND FOR OVER 32 YEARS.

LIBRARY OF CONGRESS CATALOGING-IN-PUBLICATION DATA
RABOFF, ERNEST LLOYD
    PAUL GAUGUIN
    (ART FOR CHILDREN)
REPRINT. ORIGINALLY PUBLISHED: GARDEN CITY, N.Y.: DOUBLEDAY, 1974. SUMMARY: A BRIEF BIOGRAPHY OF PAUL GAUGUIN ACCOMPANIES FIFTEEN COLOR REPRODUCTIONS AND CRITICAL INTERPRETATIONS OF HIS WORKS. 1. GAUGUIN, PAUL, 1848-1903 - JUVENILE LITERATURE. 2. PAINTERS - FRANCE - BIOGRAPHY - JUVENILE LITERATURE. 3. GAUGUIN, PAUL, 1848-1903 - CRITICISM AND INTERPRETATION - JUVENILE LITERATURE. 4. PAINTING, FRENCH - JUVENILE LITERATURE. 5. PAINTING, MODERN - 19TH CENTURY - FRANCE - JUVENILE LITERATURE. [1. GAUGUIN, PAUL, 1848-1903. 2. ARTISTS. 3. PAINTING, FRENCH. 4. PAINTING, MODERN. 5. ART APPRECIATION] I. GAUGUIN, PAUL, 1848-1903. II. TITLE III. SERIES: ART FOR CHILDREN.
ND553.G27R23   1988   759.4   [92]   87-16914   ISBN 0-397-32225-9

PAUL GAUGUIN

By Ernest Raboff

ART
FOR
CHILDREN

J. B. LIPPINCOTT · NEW YORK

PAUL GAUGUIN

WAS BORN IN PARIS ON JUNE 7, 1848 . HIS FATHER, CLOVIS GAUGUIN, WAS A JOURNALIST. HIS MOTHER , ALINE , WAS THE DAUGHTER OF FLORA TRISTAN , A FAMOUS WRITER.

AFTER HIS FATHER'S DEATH, PAUL AND HIS MOTHER SPENT FOUR YEARS IN LIMA , PERU . AT THE AGE OF SEVEN HE RETURNED TO FRANCE TO BEGIN HIS SCHOOLING. LATER, HE SPENT SEVERAL YEARS AS A SAILOR BEFORE GOING TO WORK IN A PARIS BANK AS A STOCK BROKER.

IN 1873 , AT THE AGE OF TWENTY FIVE HE MARRIED METTE GAAD , WHO WAS DANISH. THEY HAD FIVE CHILDREN IN THE NEXT TEN YEARS. AT THIS SAME TIME , HE BECAME FRIENDLY WITH ARTISTS AND BEGAN TO PAINT. AMONG THE NOW FAMOUS PAINTERS HE KNEW WERE PISSARRO , BERNARD , VAN GOGH AND DEGAS.

DURING A FINANCIAL DEPRESSION IN 1883 , GAUGUIN LOST HIS JOB AND WAS FORCED TO MOVE HIS FAMILY TO DENMARK. HE RETURNED TO PARIS DETERMINED TO BECOME A PROFESSIONAL PAINTER. FIRST HE JOINED THE IMPRESSIONISTS. THEN, INFLUENCED BY JAPANESE ART, HE DEVELOPED HIS OWN STYLE.

SEEKING A SIMPLE , NATURAL WAY OF LIFE , HE LIVED OUT HIS YEARS ON ISLANDS OF THE SOUTH PACIFIC. HIS PAINTINGS ARE BEAUTIFUL STUDIES OF THE LANDSCAPE AND THE PEACEFUL WAYS OF THE PEOPLE .

PORTRAIT OF THE ARTIST BY ERNEST RABOFF

PAUL GAUGUIN

WROTE: "TO DRAW FREELY IS NOT TO LIE
TO ONESELF."

"LIFE IS HARDLY MORE THAN A FRACTION OF A SECOND.
SUCH A LITTLE TIME TO PREPARE ONESELF FOR ETERNITY."

ACHILLE DE LA ROCHE, THE FAMOUS ART CRITIC, WROTE:
"GAUGUIN IS THE PAINTER OF PRIMITIVE NATURES; HE
LOVES THEM AND POSSESSES THEIR SIMPLICITY."

"FROM THESE HUMAN FIGURES, THIS BLAZING FLORA,
THE FANTASTIC AND THE MARVELOUS SPRING FORTH..."
"...AN ENCHANTING MAGIC OF COLOR...
THE TONES CONTRAST OR MELT INTO ONE
ANOTHER IN GRADATIONS THAT SING
LIKE A SYMPHONY..."

VINCENT VAN GOGH WROTE:
"GAUGUIN IS VERY POWERFUL,
STRONGLY CREATIVE, AND BECAUSE
OF THAT HE MUST HAVE PEACE
HE IS A VERY GREAT ARTIST AND
VERY INTERESTING AS A FRIEND."

(GO-GAN)

STAFF CLUB, POLYNESIA
MUSEUM OF PRIMITIVE ART, NEW YORK

"PORTRAIT OF THE ARTIST WITH THE IDOL" SHOWS
US THE ARTIST AS HE PAINTED HIMSELF, THINKING
PERHAPS OF HIS FUTURE YEARS IN THE SOUTH PACIFIC.

HIS EYES LOOK PAST US. HE SEEMS TO DREAM OF
DISTANT LANDS; CRADLING HIS CHIN, HIS HAND RESTS ON
HIS BLUE-DOTTED WHITE SCARF AND BOLDLY STRIPED
ORANGE SWEATER.

NOTICE HOW THE TROPICAL GREEN COLORS ARE USED ON
THE IDOL, THE COAT, THE SMOOTHED HAIR, IN THE WALL
AND ARE REFLECTED ON THE SKIN OF HIS FACE AND HAND.

THE BACK OF HIS CHAIR GLOWS LIKE A GOLDEN SUN.

IN ALL OF PAUL GAUGUIN'S PAINTINGS THERE IS
A CALM, A PEACE, THAT SHOWS THE CONTENTMENT
HE FOUND IN HIS WORK. HE TELLS US THAT WORK
WE LOVE BRINGS US HAPPINESS.

LE SOURIRE (THE SMILE)   NATIONAL GALLERY OF ART, WASHINGTON D.C., ROSENWALD COLLECTION

PORTRAIT OF THE ARTIST WITH THE IDOL   MC NAY ART INSTITUTE, SAN ANTONIO, TEXAS

"THE SEINE AT THE IENA BRIDGE" WAS PAINTED
BY GAUGUIN WHEN HE WAS 27 YEARS OLD.

FOUR YEARS EARLIER, GAUGUIN HAD MET EMILE SCHUFFENECKER
THE ARTIST WHO INSPIRED HIS INTEREST IN ART AND WAS
HIS FIRST PAINTING TEACHER.

THIS EARLY, MASTERFUL WORK IS LIKE A MAGIC CARPET.
WE ARE CARRIED ONTO THE SNOW-COVERED QUAY TOWARD A
CLOAKED MAN WHO IS WALKING ALONG THE RIVER'S BANK.

METTE-SOPHIE
COURTAULD INSTITUTE GALLERIES, LONDON

TO THE RIGHT, A MAN BENDS OVER A
FIRE ON THE GROUND. FROM THIS
WE FOLLOW MOORING LINES
PAST TWO MORE DARK FIGURES TO
TWO BARGES RESTING BEHIND THE
LARGE BULKY HOUSEBOAT WITH
ITS TALL SMOKING CHIMNEY.
THE BOAT'S SHINING ROOF REFLECTS
THE COLD WINTER SKY AND
LEADS US UP THE CONCRETE WALLS
TO THE TREE-LINED BANK
ABOVE THE RIVER.

THE SLOPING BLUE HILLS AND
THE SKY WITH ITS SINGLE PINK
CLOUD MOVE US ON TO THE ARCHED
BRIDGE. WE SKIP PAST THE
BOAT PUFFING SMOKE LIKE WHITE
BREATH IN THE CHILL WINTER AIR.

ON THE OPPOSITE BANK, FROM BUILDINGS, SPIRES AND TREES WE
PASS DOWN THE STONE STEPS TO THE QUAY WITH ITS ANCHORED
BOATS AND RETURN ACROSS THE SEINE TO OUR STARTING POINT.
OUR MAGICAL TOUR OF THE PAINTING IS COMPLETED.

THE SEINE AT THE IENA BRIDGE   THE LOUVRE, PARIS

"SCENE AT THE PORT OF DIEPPE" IS A WORK
CREATED TWO YEARS AFTER GAUGUIN BECAME A FULL-TIME ARTIST.

THE ARTIST TOOK MANY SEA VOYAGES IN HIS LIFETIME
AND OFTEN VISITED FRENCH PORTS LIKE THIS ONE.

BOATS WERE BOTH HOMES AND CHURCHES FOR THOSE WHO
LIVED OR TRAVELED ON THE SEAS. HERE GAUGUIN'S WOODEN
MASTS RISE HIGH IN THE SKY LIKE CATHEDRAL STEEPLES.

THE MULTI-HUED CLOUDS, THE SKY, HARBOR WALLS, MEADOWS
AND MASTS ARE FLOODED WITH WARM COLOR REFLECTED FROM

THE SUNLIGHT.
AGAINST THIS BRIGHT
SETTING WE SEE THE
PORT BUILDINGS AND
THE GRACEFUL BOATS
AT ANCHOR IN THE
SHIMMERING
WATER.

IF WE WILL
LOOK
CAREFULLY,
GAUGUIN WROTE,
WE WILL "...ENJOY
ENDLESS
PLEASURE..."

NEGRESS   VAN GOGH MUSEUM, AMSTERDAM

SCENE AT THE PORT OF DIEPPE   CITY ART GALLERY, MANCHESTER, ENGLAND

"BRETON PEASANT GIRLS" IS AN EXAMPLE OF GAUGUIN'S IMPRESSIONIST PERIOD OF PAINTING. SHORT STROKES OF DIFFERENT COLORS ARE PLACED NEXT TO EACH OTHER TO IMITATE HOW COLOR APPEARS IN NATURE.

STUDY ALL THE COLORS IN THE WHITE HEADDRESS AND STARCHED LINEN COLLAR ON THE GIRL IN THE MIDDLE. DISCOVER HOW THE ARTIST PAINTS HER BLOUSE AND SKIRT TO REPEAT THE COLORS OF THE GARDEN, EARTH AND SKY. THESE SAME COLORS ARE AGAIN REFLECTED IN THE BROWN GARDEN WALL.

THE GIRL ON THE RIGHT LEANS AGAINST THE WALL AND QUIETLY ADJUSTS HER SHOE AS SHE LISTENS. HER LONG FLOWER-PATTERNED GREEN APRON, BROWN BLOUSE AND BLUE SKIRT LEAD OUR EYES UP THE LEAFY TREE AND PAST ANOTHER GARDEN WALL TO THE BUSY FARMER.

THE THIRD GIRL'S HEAD DIRECTS OUR ATTENTION TO THE GEESE IN THE MEADOW AND TO THE WOMAN IN THE RED SKIRT WHO APPEARS TO BE TELLING SOME SERIOUS NEWS.

BRETON GIRLS DANCING   GEMEENTE MUSEA, AMSTERDAM

BRETON PEASANT GIRLS

"LANDSCAPE NEAR ARLES" WAS PAINTED WHILE PAUL GAUGUIN WAS LIVING IN THIS SMALL VILLAGE IN THE SOUTH OF FRANCE WITH HIS FRIEND, VINCENT VAN GOGH.

PAUL AND VINCENT RESPECTED EACH OTHER AS PAINTERS AND WORKED SIDE BY SIDE IN ARLES. THE WARM CLIMATE ALLOWED THEM TO STUDY AND TO PAINT COLORS AGAIN AND AGAIN AS THEY CHANGED WITH THE MOVING SUNLIGHT. THE TWO FRIENDS TALKED ABOUT ART CONSTANTLY. THEY STUDIED THE MASTERS OF THEIR DAY AND WROTE FASCINATING PAPERS ABOUT PAINTING AND COLOR.

THEY ADMIRED AND WERE INFLUENCED BY THE GREAT JAPANESE WOODCUT ARTISTS. GAUGUIN LOOKED FOR THE SIMPLE WAY OF LIFE HE FOUND IN THE ART OF THE JAPANESE AND IN THE WORK OF EARLY PRIMITIVE TYPE ARTISTS. HE SOUGHT A PERSONAL VISION, A UNIQUE WAY OF SEEING, DIFFERENT FROM ALL OTHERS, JUST AS ONE'S PERSONALITY AND ONE'S FINGER PRINTS ARE DIFFERENT FROM OTHERS.

THIS PAINTING OF FIELDS NEAR ARLES, OF SUNLIT HAYSTACK, FARM BUILDINGS AND PATTERNED SKY BEGINS TO SHOW THE GENTLE, POETIC FORMS AND STRIKING COLOR COMBINATIONS WHICH BECAME UNIQUELY GAUGUIN'S AND WHICH LATER BROUGHT HIM FAME.

L'ARLESIENNE   COLLECTION OF DR. AND MRS. T. E. HANLEY, BRADFORD, PENNSYLVANIA

LANDSCAPE NEAR ARLES

"BONJOUR, MONSIEUR GAUGUIN"... "GOOD MORNING, MISTER GAUGUIN," SAYS THE YOUNG WOMAN AS THE ARTIST APPROACHES HER FENCE ON HIS EARLY MORNING WALK WITH HIS SMALL DOG. IT IS A CHILLY DAY AND BOTH OF THEM ARE BUNDLED IN WRAPS AGAINST THE COLD AIR.

GAUGUIN WEARS A BERET PULLED DOWN OVER HIS EAR AND A LONG, CAPED, RED COAT THAT ALMOST REACHES TO HIS WOODEN SHOES. WE CAN SEE A WARM SWEATER AND TROUSERS UNDER THE CAPE.

THE WOMAN WEARS A SHOULDER-LENGTH BROWN HOOD ON HER HEAD AND HER FULL BLUE ROBE WITH THE APRON IN FRONT, FALLS TO THE TOPS OF HER SHOES.

BEHIND THE TWO FIGURES, THE THIN TREES ARE BARE OF LEAVES. THE DULL GREEN AND FADED ORANGE OF THE FLAT FIELDS SHOW THAT WINTER IS NEAR

A COOL, PALE SUN RISES OVER THE ROOF OF A DISTANT BARN. THE GRAY-BLUE SKY IS FILLED WITH CLOUDS THAT LOOK LIKE THE GRAY ROCKS AT THE END OF THE FENCE.

NOTICE THE SINGLE STRIP OF BRIGHT YELLOW FIELDS.

GAUGUIN KNEW HOW TO MAKE WARM COLORS BRIGHTEN A BLEAK DAY.

DESIGN FOR A PLATE   MAISON GIRAUDON, PARIS

BONJOUR, MONSIEUR GAUGUIN   NATIONAL GALLERY, PRAGUE

"WE GREET THEE, MARY" IS A RICH COLOR SONG THAT TELLS A STORY. USING FLAT FORMS OF COLOR LIKE THE JAPANESE WOOD-BLOCK PRINTS WHICH HE STUDIED, GAUGUIN SHOWS US THAT HE REGARDED MOTHERS AS MADONNAS.

SOFTLY SMILING MARY AND HER RESTING CHILD HAVE HALOS AROUND THEIR HEADS. WE CAN ALMOST FEEL THE GLOW OF NATURAL AFFECTION FROM THE TWO BODIES AS THE MOTHER PROTECTIVELY HOLDS HER SON TO HER.

IN THE CENTER OF THE PICTURE STAND TWO ADORING WOMEN WITH HANDS CLASPED. BEHIND THEM A GUARDIAN ANGEL STANDS. HER GOLDEN WINGS AND SOFT ROBE, LIKE THE BLUE AND PINK OF THE LANDSCAPE, CONTRAST WITH MARY'S VIBRANT RED GOWN.

THE FIGURES IN THE PAINTING STAND ON MULTI-COLORED BANDS OF ISLAND LANDSCAPE. BEGINNING WITH GREEN AT THE BOTTOM EDGE BELOW THE MADONNA, WE NEXT SEE BLUE, RICH BROWN, PINK-GOLD AND THE TROPICAL BLUE OF THE SKY AND MOUNTAIN.

THE COLOR-FLOODED SETTING OF WHITE AND RED FLOWERING TREES, BLOSSOMING BUSHES AND FRESH-PLUCKED FRUITS MAKE THIS SOUTH PACIFIC SCENE SEEM LIKE A LUSH PARADISE.

GAUGUIN'S COLOR SONG IS A HAPPY AND PEACEFUL ONE.

IA ORANA MARIA

WE GREET THEE, MARY   METROPOLITAN MUSEUM, NEW YORK   SAMUEL A. LEWISOHN BEQUEST

IN "THE POOR FISHERMAN" GAUGUIN SHOWS US THE BASIC ELEMENTS OF AN ISLAND FISHERMAN'S LIFE — HIS HANDMADE BOAT AND THE SEA.

THE RESTING FISHERMAN SITS THOUGHTFULLY AFTER HIS DAY'S WORK. HE SIPS REFRESHMENT FROM A COCONUT SHELL. SHADED FROM THE SUN, HIS BODY, THE SLENDER CRAFT AND THE PEBBLED SAND TAKE ON RICHER AND DEEPER TONES. THE EMERALD GREEN SEA AND THE THATCHED ROOF REFLECT YELLOW FROM THE GOLDEN SUNSET IN THE SKY.

THE FEW WHITE CAPS AND FLUNG SPUME AT THE BASE OF THE TOWERING SEA WALL ARE PEACEFUL CURLS ON THE FACE OF THE WATER.

GAUGUIN USED LARGE BLOCKS OF BOLD COLORS TO MAKE A STRONG, SIMPLE STATEMENT ABOUT ISLAND LIFE.

NOTICE THE ROLLING GREEN SEA, THE BLUE BOAT, THE MUSCULAR, BROWNED MAN AND THE RUST-RED EARTH.

THE FISHERMEN'S LIVES DEPEND ON THE SEA. FOR THEM IT IS BOTH FRUITFUL AND DANGEROUS.

CERAMIC VASE   DANISH MUSEUM OF DECORATIVE ARTS, COPENHAGEN

THE POOR FISHERMAN   SAO PAULO MUSEUM, BRAZIL

"TA MATETE" MEANS THE MARKET PLACE.

PAUL GAUGUIN LOVED THE SIMPLE WAY OF LIFE HE FOUND ON THE ISLANDS OF THE SOUTH PACIFIC OCEAN. THE MARKET PLACE OF THE VILLAGES WAS NOT ONLY WHERE THE PEOPLE SHOPPED, IT WAS THE CENTER OF THEIR SOCIAL LIFE.

THE LADIES COULD WEAR THEIR PRETTIEST DRESSES AND ENJOY A FEW HOURS WITH FRIENDS AWAY FROM THEIR FAMILY CHORES.

THE BUSY AND COLORFUL MARKET PLACE WAS ALWAYS OUTDOORS AND CLOSE TO THE WATER, WHICH WAS VERY IMPORTANT TO ALL OF THEIR LIVES.

HOW PLEASANT TO SIT AND SHOP BENEATH THE SHADY TREES, TO TALK WITH FRIENDS NEAR COOL GREEN GRASS, TO WATCH THE MEN CARRYING IN THEIR FRESH FISH ON LONG POLES, TO RELAX BY THE RUSHING SEA AND ENJOY ALL THE ACTIVITY.

THE ARTIST PAINTED THESE BEAUTIFUL WOMEN ALMOST LIKE THE EGYPTIAN PRINCESSES WERE PAINTED IN EGYPT'S VERY OLD PYRAMIDS.

STEPHANE MALLARME   MUSEUM OF MODERN ART, NEW YORK

TA MATETE (THE MARKET)   KUNSTMUSEUM, BASEL

"THE MOON AND THE EARTH" LIKE MANY GREAT WORKS OF ART
IS FILLED WITH SYMBOLIC MEANING. GAUGUIN HAS COMBINED
SYMBOLS FROM ISLAND LEGENDS AND MYTHS OF THE SOUTH
SEAS WITH HIS OWN EUROPEAN BELIEFS TO TELL THIS STORY.

THE WOMAN WITH HER STRONG FEET FIRMLY ON THE GROUND AND
ARMS CURVING UPWARD TOWARD THE MAN-FIGURE REPRESENTS
THE MOON. HER FACE IS SILHOUETTED AGAINST A WHITE CRESCENT.

THE OVER-SIZED MAN BEYOND HER, MASSIVE AND PROTECTIVE,
SYMBOLIZES THE RICH BROWN EARTH. HE IS PROVIDER, HUSBAND AND FATHER.

GAUGUIN WROTE, "MAN LOVES WOMAN IF HE HAS UNDERSTOOD WHAT
A MOTHER IS...MAN LOVES WOMAN IF HE HAS UNDERSTOOD WHAT A CHILD
IS." THE PAINTING SEEMS TO SHOW THE ARTIST'S GREAT RESPECT
FOR NATURE'S SIMPLE FORMULA FOR LIFE AND CREATION.

EDGAR DEGAS, THE NOTED FRENCH PAINTER, RECOGNIZED THIS
WORK AS A MASTERPIECE AND BOUGHT IT IN 1893, THE YEAR IT WAS PAINTED.

Paul Gauguin

Les Cigales et les fourmie

THE GRASSHOPPERS AND THE ANTS   NATIONAL GALLERY OF ART, WASHINGTON D.C., ROSENWALD COLLECTION

THE MOON AND THE EARTH   MUSEUM OF MODERN ART, NEW YORK, LILLIE P. BLISS COLLECTION

IN "TAHITIAN LANDSCAPE" OUR EYES SWEEP FROM GOLDEN FOREGROUND TO TOWERING RED MOUNTAIN.

WHAT A FEELING OF PEACE AND HARMONY GAUGUIN HAS CREATED WITH HIS SUNLIT MEADOWS, COLORFUL TREES, BRIGHT SHRUBS AND SOARING MOUNTAIN.

NOA NOA (FRAGRANCE) MUSEUM OF MODERN ART, NEW YORK
LILLIE P. BLISS COLLECTION

FROM THE TWO BROAD PINK FOOTPATHS AT THE BOTTOM OF THE LANDSCAPE, WE SEE THE STRAW-HATTED MAN BALANCING TWO BUNCHES OF FRUIT ON HIS CARRYING POLE. BEYOND HIM WE FOLLOW THE GREEN SHRUBS TO THE BLACK DOG AT THE LEFT, PASS THE LAYERED TROPICAL GROWTHS AND ARE REMINDED OF HOW TALL THE GRACEFUL PALM TREES ARE AND HOW HIGH THE MOUNTAIN RISES.

THE PAINTING IS FILLED WITH THE BRIGHT AND EXOTIC COLORS OF TAHITI. BUT THEY ARE CHOSEN AND COMBINED IN A WAY UNIQUE TO GAUGUIN. WE RECOGNIZE HIS PAINTING AS BOTH REAL AND FANCIFUL.

THE ARTIST PAINTED THIS SCENE JUST FIVE MONTHS AFTER HIS ARRIVAL IN TAHITI. HE WROTE HOME TO FRANCE: "I FEEL ALL OF THIS PENETRATING ME AND NOW CAN REST IN EXTRAORDINARY FASHION."

HEAD OF A TAHITIAN WOMAN   CLEVELAND MUSEUM OF ART,
MR. AND MRS. LEWIS B. WILLIAMS COLLECTION

"AREAREA" (RECREATION) IS AN EXAMPLE OF THE GENTLE WAY OF LIFE THAT GAUGUIN SOUGHT IN TAHITI.

THE LARGE ORANGE DOG PLAYS IN THE GRASS IN FRONT OF THE TWO WOMEN. THEY REST ON THE GROUND BENEATH A SHADE TREE SURROUNDED BY FLOWERS AND GRACEFUL TROPICAL PLANTS. NOTICE HOW THE COLORS CHANGE IN THE SUNLIGHT.

THE GIRL IN THE BLUE SKIRT PLAYS A TUNE ON HER REED PIPE. HER FRIEND LISTENS WITH PLEASURE AND OBSERVES THE SCENE BEFORE HER. BEYOND THE BRIGHTLY COLORED PATCHES OF EARTH, OTHER GAILY DRESSED MAIDENS APPEAR TO BE PRAYING TO AN ISLAND GODDESS. PRAYER WAS A DAILY PART OF THE NATIVES' LIVES WHICH GAUGUIN RECORDED IN THIS RESTFUL SCENE.

PAUL GAUGUIN LOVED THESE SIMPLE PEOPLE.

HE SPENT THE MOST PRODUCTIVE YEARS OF HIS PAINTING CAREER, LIVING AMONG THEM, TRYING TO CAPTURE THEIR EASY WAYS AND THEIR PRIMITIVE BEAUTY.

AREAREA (RECREATION)   THE LOUVRE, PARIS

SACRED MOUNTAIN   COLLECTION MR. AND MRS. RODOLPHE MEYER DE SCHAUENSEE, DEVON, PENNSYLVANIA